DISGUISES
You Can Make

DISGUISES
You Can Make

by EVE BARWELL

illustrated by RICHARD ROSENBLUM

Lothrop, Lee & Shepard Company
A Division of William Morrow & Co., Inc. • New York

Books by Eve Barwell

Make Your Pet a Present
Disguises You Can Make

1   2   3   4   5   6   7   8   9   10

Library of Congress Cataloging in Publication Data
Barwell, Eve.
    Disguises you can make.
    SUMMARY: Step-by-step instructions for twenty-four basic disguises plus
variations using common craft materials and makeup.
    1. Children—Clothing—Juvenile literature.
2. Costume—Juvenile literature.   3. Make-up,
Theatrical—Juvenile literature.   [1. Costume.
2. Makeup, Theatrical]   I. Rosenblum, Richard.
II. Title.
TT649.B37   792'.026   77-24998
ISBN 0-688-41810-4
ISBN 0-688-51810-9 lib. bdg.

CONTENTS

INTRODUCTION

Have you ever wished you were someone else? You have? With this book, you can have the very next best thing—a disguise so foolproof that even your own family won't know you.

A disguise can consist of a mask or a painted face, perhaps with a false beard or moustache. Begin by reading the opening chapter which describes the many easily-available materials you can use. It also gives hints on moustaches, beards, scars, and other finishing touches. And, for those who want to look really professional, there are tips about theatrical supplies and makeup.

When choosing a disguise, do not automatically pick one of the same sex as yourself. If you are a boy, you might choose to disguise yourself as a pirate, but you could also become an old woman. If you are a girl, why not try the devil disguise, instead of the china doll. They might be slightly more difficult, but they would be more likely to baffle even your best friend.

One last piece of advice: remember to think yourself into the disguise. Convince yourself that you are the creature or person, and walk or talk as they would do. It will make all the difference.

MATERIALS

It is possible to make an excellent disguise with the simplest of materials—newspaper, cardboard, yarn, paints, and ordinary makeup. This chapter will describe just some of the many possibilities open to you. And since a book of disguises would not be complete without mentioning greasepaint and other theatrical supplies, a word or two has been included on how to use them. These items, which you may find more difficult to obtain, and which are not essential to the disguises in this book, have been marked with an asterisk. (To find stores in your area which carry theatrical supplies, look in the Yellow Pages under "Cosmetics," "Costumes," "Theatrical Equipment and Supplies," and "Theatrical Makeup.")

Before you begin your disguises, it is a good idea to gather all the necessary materials together and read through the directions. If any gluing or painting is involved, be sure you protect your work surface with plenty of newspaper.

• FOR MEASURING

You will need a ruler, yardstick, or tape measure for many of the disguises. All measurements in this book are given in both inches and centimeters. Choose which measuring system you prefer *before* you begin—do not switch from one system to the other.

For a few of the disguises you will need to draw circles. Sometimes it is possible to draw around a saucer or plate, but a compass is best for the Owl disguise. Of course, you can always draw the circles freehand, or you can make a substitute compass using string with a pencil tied to one end, and a thumbtack on the other. The length of the string should be the same as the radius (half the diameter) of the circle you need. Tack the string to the center of the piece of cardboard or paper then, keeping the string taut, hold the pencil upright and draw the circle (see illustration).

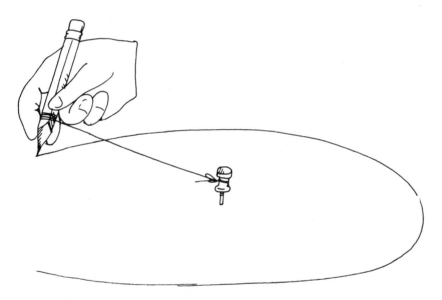

• FOR CUTTING

Scissors are needed for most of the disguises. Choose the size that is easiest for you to handle. Sharp-pointed scissors are necessary for those disguises where hole-punching is required.

• FOR FASTENING

Glue: Select any nontoxic, white glue, such as Elmer's or Sobo's. These will glue almost anything to anything else, and turn clear as they dry. Nontoxic, white glue has the added advantage of being easy to wash off brushes and clothing.

Tape: Most of the tape used in this book is regular cellophane tape. However, it is possible to substitute masking or adhesive tape for many of the disguises. Test a substitute tape on the material you will be fastening before you begin the disguise.

Flour-and-water paste: You can make this by mixing 1 heaping tablespoon of flour with 2 tablespoons of cold water, and adding ½ cup of boiling water. Stir it well, and add a bit more flour if it is too runny.

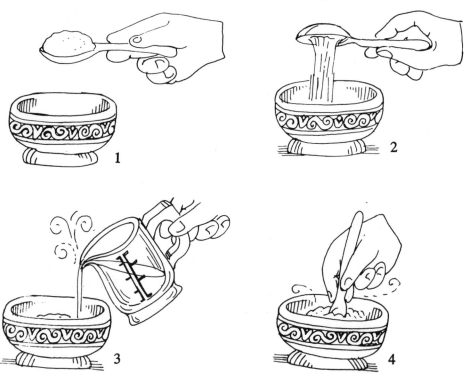

Double-sided cellophane tape: This is sometimes used for attaching beards or moustaches. Use small pieces of tape, and press them onto the reverse of the material before peeling off the protective backing from the second sticky side. Then simply press the beard or moustache in place.

*Spirit gum: Used in the theater for attaching beards and moustaches, spirit gum may be bought from theatrical suppliers and large drugstores. It usually comes with its own brush inside the bottle. To attach a moustache, first wipe your upper lip free of any grease, then spread spirit gum on both the moustache and your lip. Wait a minute or two, and then press the moustache in place. Remove spirit gum with rubbing alcohol.

Ask an adult to help you when using these materials. Use them very sparingly, and be very careful not to knock the bottles over. *Do not leave them where they might fall into the hands of very young children.*

• FOR PAINTING

Poster paint: This is the best kind of paint to use on paper, or on papier-maché masks after they have been allowed to dry. Mix them in old saucers or lids, and wash the brush in water after using each color.

Powder paint: This is a very economical paint for covering large areas. To make into a liquid, put a heaping teaspoon of powder paint into a mixing dish, add a teaspoon of water, and stir to a smooth paste with your brush. Use a different mixing dish for each color.

11

Model enamel: This dries to a bright, shiny finish. Use it for painting plastic or metal, and stir it with a toothpick before using. Clean the brush in turpentine afterward.

Water-base or latex paint: This kind of paint is usually used for painting walls, but you will find it very useful as an opaque base coat. Use it on plastic, metal, cardboard cartons, or homemade cardboard (see p. 13) to cover any writing or newsprint. You can mix poster paint with it to make pastel colors, or let it dry and then paint over it with poster paints. Wash the brushes and mixing saucers in cold water before the paint has a chance to dry on them.

• PAPER

Many of the disguises in this book need large sheets of colored cardboard or construction paper. If these are difficult to get hold of, remember that you can easily transform white cardboard to any color with a coat of paint.

Newspaper can be turned into a good substitute for thin cardboard. Just paste all the pages together with flour-and-water paste (see p. 10), and let them dry. A coat of water-base paint will help cover the newsprint, and make it ready for painting with poster paint.

• HAIR AND BEARD SUPPLIES

Hair colors: Do not use hair dyes or rinses. You may wish to try a different disguise tomorrow, and they are much too permanent. Make a wig instead or cover your hair with a suitable cap, hat, or scarf.

For an "old age" disguise, turn your hair grey or white by powdering it with talcum powder. Remove it by brushing.

Cotton: This is good for white hair, beards, and eyebrows. A small package may be bought quite cheaply from a drugstore, or any cosmetic or first aid department. Be sure you buy the kind that comes in large sheets, and not in little balls.

Lamb's wool: Often used for shoe padding, this is excellent for beards and moustaches because it has the appearance of soft, fine hair. It, too, may be found in drugstores, or any store that carries footwear supplies.

*Crepe hair: This may be bought by the yard or part of a yard from a theatrical supplier. Ask for the woolen variety and not the more expensive human hair. It comes in a thin, tight braid, and stretches out into a much

13

longer piece when unbraided. Six inches should be enough for most disguises. The hair retains the kinks from braiding, and needs to be straightened by dipping it in warm water and then winding it tightly around a jar or can to dry. Use it for beards, moustaches, and eyebrows as well as wigs.

• MAKEUP

Most women have odd pieces of makeup that they don't use anymore tucked away at the back of a drawer, so ask all your female friends and relations if they would like to contribute to your disguises box. But be sure to *ask*. People can be very possessive about makeup they

14

actually use, even if it does look a bit old and battered to you. If no one wants to donate to your good cause, check the makeup counters in drugstores and discount stores. There are many low-cost brands available.

Some people have allergic reactions to makeup. To make sure that you will not have any problems, apply a little of the makeup on the underside of your forearm the day before, and leave it on for several hours. If it makes your skin itch or look pink or blotchy, then it would not be safe to use that particular brand of make-up on your face. Ask at a drugstore, or any cosmetic counter, for one of the brands especially designed for sensitive skin.

What to look for: Do not think that eye shadow can only be used on eyelids, or lipstick on lips, for eye shadow can be used all over your face, and lipstick can be used to redden your cheeks or nose or make the marks on a clown's face. Whatever makeup you are given, think of it as a color, rather than as an item for use on only one part of your face.

Makeup foundation comes in many shades of pink, beige, or brown. Use it as an all-over face color to make you look extra pale or tanned.

If you are uncertain about which brand of makeup to buy, select the kind which seems non-greasy and easiest to apply (and remove). In general, the liquid and cream makeups are easier and less messy to use than the powdered ones.

Cold cream: Whatever makeup you are planning to use, it is best to rub a little cold cream into your skin

15

first. It will stop the makeup from sinking into your pores, and makes it easier to remove afterward.

Cold cream is the best remover for ordinary makeup or greasepaint. Spread it on liberally with your fingers, and then wipe it away with cotton or tissues.

*Greasepaint: Theatrical greasepaint is sometimes sold in tubes, but generally in sticks like large wax crayons. It comes in all shades of beige, brown, and pink, as well as black, and a wide selection of bright colors.

When using greasepaint, first wash and dry your face, and rub in a little cold cream. Remove any excess cream with a tissue. When using it as a foundation color, mark stripes of greasepaint down your face, and spread the color over your skin with your fingers until it is evenly blended. For stronger colors, as for a clown's disguise, fill in the areas as if you are coloring a picture with a crayon.

Actors pat a layer of transparent powder over their greasepaint to "fix" it, and make it look less shiny, but this is a step you can easily omit.

Remove greasepaint with liberal amounts of cold cream, which can be wiped away with tissues or cotton.

Finger paints: These are thick, nontoxic, cream paints sold in large plastic bottles for use without paintbrushes. Test them on your arm the day before, as suggested for regular makeup. Paint them onto your face with your finger, and remove them with lots of soap and water.

*Nose putty: This is sold in a small, hard stick, like greasepaint. It can be used for all sorts of things—false noses or altering the shape of a nose, warts, covering up eyes or eyebrows, or making ears stick out. Break off a small piece and work it between your fingers until it is really soft and pliable, like very soft plasticine or Play Doh. (Mix in a little Vaseline or cold cream, if necessary.) Wipe your skin clean of grease or makeup, and the putty should stick to it without any kind of adhesive. If it doesn't stick, glue it on with spirit gum.

To remove a false nose made of putty, hold a small piece of string or thread quite taut, and drag it down the bridge of your nose. Or rub it with cold cream until it comes away easily.

Plasticine: You can use plasticine in the same way as nose putty. Work it between your fingers to make it as soft as you can, form it into the shape you want, and glue it on with spirit gum. To remove it, simply lift off the plasticine nose or warts, and get rid of any remaining traces of gum with a little rubbing alcohol on a piece of cotton.

*Collodion: The non-flexible variety, bought from a theatrical supplier, is ideal for making scars. It has its own brush in the bottle. Paint a line of collodion down one cheek, and watch it wrinkle up like a scar as it dries. Remove it with rubbing alcohol.

New-Skin: This is a good substitute for collodion. It is used for painting over tiny cuts and grazes to help them heal, and it may be bought from a drugstore. Paint a line of it down your face with the spreader provided. When it dries, open your mouth really wide so that your

17

cheek stretches. When you close your mouth again, your skin will pucker in a realistic scar. Remove it by just peeling it off gently.

• **MISCELLANEOUS EFFECTS**

Missing teeth: You can obtain this look by painting out a tooth or two with greasepaint or wax crayon. Wipe it off afterward with a tissue.

Tattoos: Look in toyshops for a packet of "painless tattoos," which apply like transfers.

CAT

Cat personalities vary almost as much as human ones. But whether you leap about like a playful kitten, or prowl and stretch like a queenly Siamese, be sure to meow, purr, and hiss like a real cat.

• MATERIALS

large, plain, two-sided paper bag, about 14 x 16 inches
  (35 x 40 cm)
black felt-tip pen
6 pieces of stiff string, 12 inches (30 cm) long
small piece of cellophane tape
sharp-pointed scissors
tape measure
thread

1. Draw a cat's face in the center of one side of the paper
   bag. Leave a 2-inch (5-cm) border all around the drawing (Figure 1). Make sure the eyes are the same distance
   apart as your own.

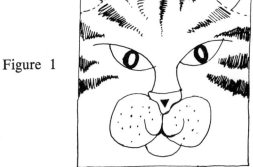

Figure 1

2. Draw dark pupils inside the slanted eyes. Cut a vertical
   slit in each so that you will be able to see (Figure 2).

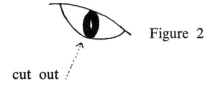

Figure 2

cut out

20

3. Cut out a small triangle just below the cat's nose for a breathing hole.
4. With closed scissors, pierce 6 small holes on each side of the nose. Thread each piece of string through one hole on each side to make whiskers. Attach them to the inside of the bag with cellophane tape.
5. Bunch up each of the two top corners of the bag to make ears. Tie them tightly with thread, and bend them slightly forward (Figure 3).

Figure 3

6. Pop the bag over your head for an instant cat disguise.

• **VARIATIONS**

Tiger: Paint the bag orange before you start, and make the black stripes darker and thicker. Make the eyes narrower, and bend the ears backward for a really mean expression.

Leopard: Make it like the tiger disguise, but draw spots instead of stripes.

Lion: Make it like the cat, but with rounder eyes. Glue a piece of wide yarn fringe (about 50 inches or 1.3 m long) under the chin and up the sides of the bag (or use strips of yarn), crossing the ends behind the ears. Or make a fringe from paper strips about 6 inches (15 cm) long and 2 inches (5 cm) wide, glued all around the face.

CHINA DOLL

A doll moves stiffly and stares and perhaps blinks very slowly. You might be the kind that can also say "Mama."

• MATERIALS

balloon that will blow up
   bigger than your head
newspaper
flour-and-water paste (see p. 10)
Vaseline
ball of thick, yellow yarn
2 pieces of brown paper,
   1½ x ¾ inches (4 x 2 cm)
   or an old pair of false eyelashes
red, white, and brown poster paints
paintbrush
tape measure
sharp-pointed scissors
stapler
glue
2 hair ribbons
jar or cup for mixing paint

23

1. Blow up the balloon to the size of your head, and tie the neck. Cover it with Vaseline.
2. Tear some newspaper into pieces about 2 inches (5 cm) square. Dip them one by one in the flour-and-water paste, and lay them on the balloon, edges overlapping (Figure 1).
3. Leaving a small space around the neck, cover the balloon with four or five layers of newspaper pieces.

Figure 1

4. Hang the balloon up by the neck, and let it dry. This will take about twenty-four hours.

5. Burst the balloon, and pull it out of the newspaper shell. Cut the shell in half to make two mask shapes. Save the other half for the Skeleton disguise (p. 99).

6. Cut out holes for the eyes, the same distance apart as your own.

7. Make a pale pink paint by mixing a few drops of red paint with the white. Paint the face of the mask with this mixture. When it is dry, paint round, deep-pink cheeks with a mixture of red and pink paints. Then add a red, cupid's-bow mouth. Draw pale brown eyebrows and long, curved eyelashes *below* the eyes. Outline the nose in the same color.

8. Along one long side of each brown paper strip, make lots of parallel cuts more than half way across to form fringe-like eyelashes. Glue them in a curve above each eye. (Or glue on a pair of old false eyelashes.) Curl the lashes upward.

9. Cut a piece of yarn 18 inches (45 cm) longer than the outer edge of the mask for the base string for the hair. Tie each end to the back of a chair.

10. Cut about fifty pieces of yarn, each 20 inches (50 cm) long. (If you have lots of patience and plenty of yarn, cut up to one hundred pieces to make really thick hair.) Fold one of the pieces in half, and pass the loop behind the base string. Thread the ends of the yarn through the loop, and pull them tight. Repeat this with the other pieces of yarn, spacing them evenly and fairly close together along the base string (Figures 2a-d).

25

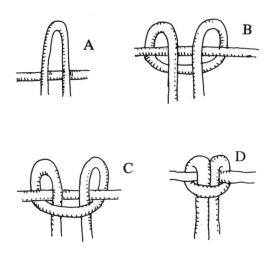

Figure 2

11. Untie the base string from the chairs, and staple it around the top and side edges of the mask to make the hair.

12. Fasten the mask to the front of your face by tying several pieces of yarn hair behind your head.

13. Tie the ribbons onto some of the side hair so that it sticks out from each side of your head. (Or attach a large bow of ribbon on top of your head with a bobby pin.)

CLOWN (happy)

Every circus clown creates his or her own individual "face." To copy those markings is a serious breach of circus manners, so try to dream up your very own design. Since you are a happy clown, you might leap gaily about, acting as if your feet and hands are so enormous that they don't really belong to you. Baggy clothes and oversize boots will help you play the part.

27

- **MATERIALS**

  mop head (available in hardware stores, or see suggested variation)

  unwaxed paper cup

  circle of cardboard, about 6 inches (15 cm) in diameter

  narrow elastic, about 20 inches (50 cm) long

  Ping-Pong ball (or bright red lipstick)

  red and black acrylic or gloss paint

  paintbrush

  soft, black eyebrow pencil (or finger paint or grease-paint *)

  talcum powder and cold cream (or white greasepaint *)

  dark, liquid makeup foundation (or brown grease-paint *)

  sharp-pointed scissors

  glue

  cotton ball

1. Glue the paper cup upside down in the center of the cardboard circle to make the hat. With closed scissors, punch a hole in the cardboard on opposite sides of the cup. Thread the elastic through each hole. Tie a large knot in both ends to form the chin strap (Figure 1).

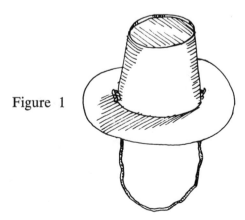

Figure 1

2. Paint the hat black, and let it dry.
3. With the scissors, cut a hole in the Ping-Pong ball so that it will just fit onto the tip of your nose. Make sure there are no jagged edges, then paint the ball red and let it dry. (Or "paint" your nose red with lipstick.)
4. Draw the outlines of the large eye and mouth shapes with black eyebrow pencil. The mouth should be extra large and turn up at the sides.
5. Cover your face outside the outlines with dark, liquid foundation or brown greasepaint.
6. Fill the areas inside the outlines with white greasepaint, or talcum powder and cold cream. If you are using talcum powder, first cover the area with a little cold cream and dab the powder on firmly with a small ball of cotton.
7. Push the Ping-Pong ball onto the end of your nose, put the mop head sideways on your head like a wig, and place the hat at a jaunty angle on top.

• **VARIATIONS**

The main ingredients for a happy face are arched eyebrows and a large mouth that turns up at the sides. Experiment with different expressions and all kinds of silly hats.

Instead of using a mop head for a wig, you could glue lots of narrow strips of paper or

29

pieces of thick yarn under the
brim of the hat, so that they
hang down like hair.

CLOWN (sad)

A sad clown is wistful and quiet and rarely speaks. Try to talk to people through mime, using your hands and facial expressions instead of your voice.

- **MATERIALS**

  sheet of stiff white paper, about 20 inches (50 cm) square
  42-inch (108-cm) strip of white paper, 6 inches (15 cm) wide
  piece of elastic, about 18 inches (46 cm) long
  small ball of black yarn (or any color you choose)
  hair net
  cold cream and talcum powder
    (or white greasepaint *)
  lipstick (or red greasepaint *)
  soft, black eyebrow pencil
    (or black greasepaint *)
  glue
  sharp-pointed scissors
  cotton ball

31

1. Roll the sheet of paper into a cone for the hat. Glue the edges, and trim the bottom into an even curve.
2. Wind the yarn around three of your fingers about fifteen times. Slip the loops off your hand, and tie them together in the center with a short piece of yarn. Cut the loops to make a pompon (Figures 1a-c).

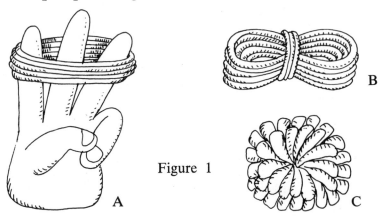

Figure 1

3. Make two more yarn pompons. Glue one to the point of the hat, and the other two at equal distances down the front.
4. With closed scissors, punch a hole in opposite sides of the hat. Thread the elastic through each hole. Tie a large knot in both ends to form the chin strap (Figure 2).

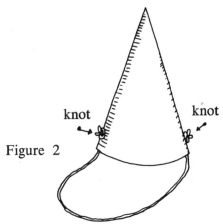

knot   knot

Figure 2

5. Pleat the strip of paper into a concertina with sections about 2 inches (5 cm) wide to make the neck ruffle. Glue the short ends together.

6. Paint your whole face white, including your eyebrows. Stop at your chin line, leaving your neck and the underside of your chin unpainted. If you are using talcum powder, rub cold cream into your skin and then dab the powder on firmly with a small ball of cotton.

7. Draw long, drooping eyebrows with eyebrow pencil or black greasepaint. Arch them higher than your own eyebrows and end them lower.

8. Draw the outline of a large, drooping mouth with black eyebrow pencil. Then, add an upside-down triangular shape which curves down each cheek. Fill in the outlines with red lipstick or greasepaint. (You will find this easier to do if you use a lip brush.)

9. Put on the hair net, and tuck all your hair inside it.

10. Slip the concertina frill over your head and, with the elastic under your chin, set the hat on at an angle.

• **VARIATIONS**

Try designing your own sad face. The only rule is that all the lines should droop and slope downward.

You could make a wig instead of a cap, starting with a Devil's skull cap (p. 41). Make three large pompons as described above, winding the yarn around a book instead of your fingers. Glue one on each side of the skull cap and one on top. To make the hair stand stiff,

spread glue on the yarn and pull the strands gently between your fingers until they dry.

DAISY

Express your feelings as a daisy
by rustling your petals with disapproval,
holding your head high with happiness,
or drooping with sadness.

• MATERIALS

circle of cardboard, 10 inches (25 cm) in diameter
1 ounce (25 gm) thick yellow yarn
2 sheets of stiff white construction paper, 26 x 20 inches
  (65 x 50 cm)
glue
old saucer
tape measure
sharp-pointed scissors
2 pieces of string, each about 18 inches (45 cm) long
flower-scented perfume (optional)

1. Cut two small eye holes in the center of the cardboard circle, the same distance apart as your own.
2. With closed scissors, punch a hole on each side of the circle, about 1 inch (2.5 cm) from the edge. Thread a piece of string through each hole and knot.
3. Wind the yarn around three of your fingers about fifteen times. Slip the loops off your fingers and cut at both ends, forming 30 pieces about 2 inches (5 cm) long. Repeat two or three more times.
4. Pour some glue into an old saucer. Dip one end of each

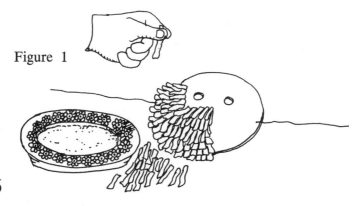

Figure 1

36

piece of yarn, one piece at a time, in the glue. Press it onto the cardboard, letting the other end hang loose. Work upward from the bottom of the circle so that the strands overlap (Figure 1). Do not worry if some of the strands hang over the eye holes—you will still be able to see through them.

5. Set this cardboard-and-yarn flower center aside to dry.

6. Fold each sheet of construction paper in quarters, and cut along the fold lines. You now have eight pieces measuring 13 x 10 inches (32.5 x 25 cm).

7. Fold each of the pieces into thirds across its width. The eight folded pieces will measure 13 x 3⅓ inches (32.5 x 8 cm). Draw a petal shape on each top layer, giving it long curved sides and blunt ends (Figure 2). Cut around the outlines through all thicknesses to make twenty-four petals.

8. Glue twelve of the petals to the wrong side of the cardboard circle. Set them side by side and equally spaced around the yarn center of the daisy.

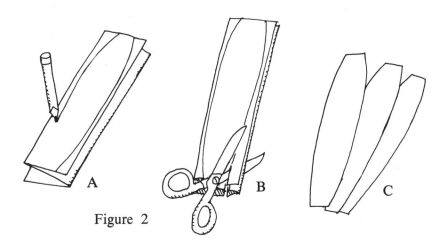

A　　　　B　　　　C

Figure 2

9. Glue the other twelve petals on top, filling the spaces between the petals in the first layer.
10. Hold the daisy in front of your face so that you can see through the eye holes. Tie the strings behind your head.
11. Spray yourself with plenty of perfume for an extra floral touch.

• VARIATIONS

Marigold: Make this in the same way, with orange yarn and orange construction paper. Use three times as many petals, and make them half as wide.

Pansy: Start with a cardboard circle, but do not cover it with pieces of yarn. Cut five large, construction-paper petals in yellow, pale purple, or reddish-brown. Paint

black markings on three of them. Glue the petals to the cardboard ring, placing three black-trimmed ones side by side. Cut eye and nose holes in the black-trimmed sections.

DEVIL

A devil has to look really evil with a thin, mean mouth and narrowed eyes. So keep your eyes half closed, and do not allow even a flicker of a smile to cross your face.

- **MATERIALS**

  red lipstick, blusher, greasepaint * or finger paint
  soft, black eyebrow pencil, black finger paint or grease-
      paint *
  newspaper
  flour-and-water paste (see page 10)
  Vaseline
  black poster paint
  2 pieces of white paper,
      about 2½ x 1½ inches
      (6 x 4 cm)
  paintbrush
  glue
  paper tissue

1. Blow up the balloon to the size of your head, or a little larger, and tie the neck. Cover the fat end opposite the neck with Vaseline.
2. Tear some newspaper into pieces about 2 inches (5 cm) square. Dip them one by one into the flour-and-water paste, and lay them on the Vaseline-covered part of the balloon, edges overlapping.
3. Cover the fat end of the balloon with four or five layers of newspaper pieces to make a skull cap shape that will come well down onto your forehead (Figure 1).

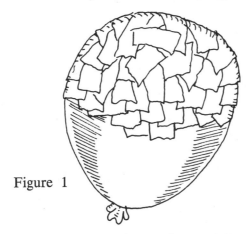

Figure 1

4. Hang the balloon up by the neck, and let it dry. This will take about twenty-four hours.
5. Burst the balloon, and throw it away. Trim the edges of the paper shape, and cut two semicircles in the front so that the cap forms a point in the center of your forehead.
6. Roll one of the pieces of white paper into a cone so that one corner of the rectangle forms the point. Glue to close, and cut straight across the open end of the cone to make it level.

41

7. Cut several small slits around the edge of the cone. Bend the pieces outward (Figure 2), and glue them to the skull cap so that the cone forms a horn.

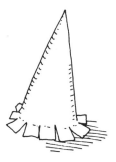

Figure 2

8. Make a second horn in the same way.
9. Paint the skull cap black, leaving the horns white.
10. Cover your whole face with red lipstick, blusher, grease-paint, or finger paint, eyebrows and all.
11. Push your hair back out of the way, and put on the skull cap.
12. Using the black eyebrow pencil, finger paint, or grease-paint, draw a triangular, pointed beard on your chin. Draw a V-shaped moustache and pointed eyebrows.

ELEPHANT

If you have ever watched an elephant, you know how very slowly you should move when wearing this disguise. Imagine how it must feel to be so heavy, then hunch your shoulders and bend forward, making the trunk swing slowly from side to side as you plod along.

43

• MATERIALS

roll of grey crepe paper, about 4 feet x 20 inches (1.30 m
 x 50 cm), or 2 sheets, each 36 x 12 inches (90 x 30
 cm)
circle of very stiff, grey cardboard (or white cardboard
 covered with grey crepe paper), 12 inches (30 cm)
 in diameter
rectangle of white cardboard, 9 x 6 inches (22 x 15 cm)
old pair of tights or pantyhose
piece of stiff wire, 36 inches (92 cm) long
cellophane tape
2 large, black buttons
glue
strong thread
sharp-pointed scissors
3 pieces of string, each 12 inches (30 cm) long
pencil or felt-tip pen

1. Make a cut from the outer edge to the center of the card-
    board circle. Overlap the cut edges 3 inches (7.5 cm),
    and glue them together. Reinforce with tape, if neces-
    sary.
2. Hold the cardboard in front of your face, overlapping
    edges pointing downward. Mark the position of the eye
    holes on each side of the center point, about 2½ inches
    (6 cm) apart. Mark the position of the base of the trunk,
    about 2 inches (5 cm) below the center point.
3. Cut slits for the eyes. Make several short cuts like the
    spokes of a wheel to hold the trunk. Cut a straight, ver-

tical slit for each tusk on each side and slightly below where the trunk will be (Figure 1).

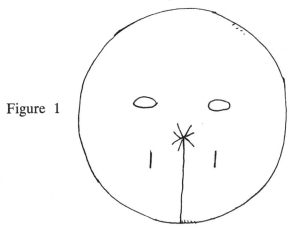

Figure 1

4. Glue a button to the outer edge of each eye slit.
5. Make a 90° bend 13 inches (33 cm) from each end of the wire. Curve the center section to follow the curve of the cardboard mask edge. Curve the outer sections more gently to make the top edges of the ears (Figure 2).

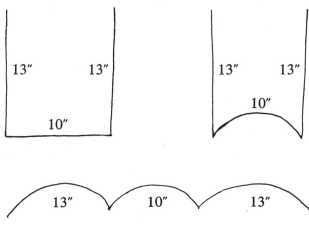

Figure 2

6. With cellophane tape, attach the middle section of the wire to the wrong side of the cardboard circle near the top.

7. For the ears, cut two pieces of crepe paper 16 x 10 inches (40 x 25 cm), with the grain of the crepe paper running across the width (the paper will "stretch" when you pull the long sides).

8. Lay the mask face down on a flat surface. Lay the ear pieces on top at an angle, so that the two inner, bottom corners meet slightly below the trunk hole, and the top edges cover the wire ear supports. Tape the edges of the crepe paper to the cardboard. Slip the top edges under the wire supports, trim off the inside corners, fold the remaining edges back over them, and fasten closed with tape (Figure 3).

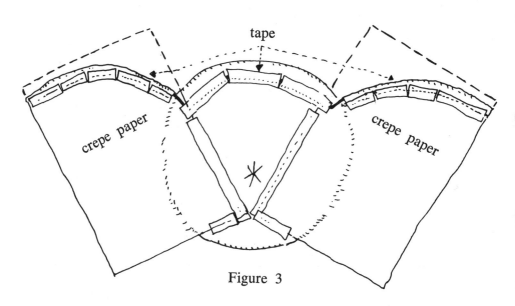

Figure 3

9. Trim the bottom edges of the ears into a curve, then gently stretch all the free edges to make them wavy and wrinkled.

10. For the trunk, cut the legs off the tights or pantyhose, and pull one leg down inside the other.

11. Cut a strip of crepe paper the length of the trunk and 8 inches (20 cm) wide. Wrap the paper around the trunk, and join the long edges with cellophane tape.

12. Push one end of the trunk through the spoked hole in the mask, and fasten it to the wrong side of the mask with tape. Tie the other end tightly with strong thread.

13. Fold the white cardboard in half, long edges together. Cut out a curved tusk shape, cutting through both thicknesses to make two matching tusks.

14. Push the tusks into the slits in the mask. Fold and tape the ends onto the back of the mask.

15. With closed scissors, punch two holes in each side of the mask, one near the edge of the cardboard face and the other alongside it and through the ear. Thread a piece of string through each pair of holes, and knot. Hold the mask in front of your face, and tie the strings behind your head.

GIRAFFE

A giraffe walks along in very stately
fashion, its head swaying backward
and forward with each stride.
Try to "walk tall"
when wearing
this disguise, and so give it
a few more inches of height.

- **MATERIALS**

  piece of stiff cardboard, 18 inches (45 cm) square (or
    sheets of newspaper pasted together—see p. 13)
  block of styrofoam, about 4 inches (10 cm) square and
    at least 2 inches (5 cm) thick
  2 bamboo garden canes, 6 feet (2 cm) long
  scraps of black and white paper or felt
  roll of brown mailing paper, at least 18 inches (45 cm)
    wide and 10 feet (3 m) long
  pencil
  sharp-pointed scissors
  glue
  yardstick
  yellow and dark brown poster paint
  paintbrush

1. Roll the large piece of cardboard into a cone-like tube,
   with a 2-inch (5-cm) opening at one end and a 5½-inch
   (14-cm) opening at the other. Glue the overlapping
   edges together.
2. Roll the cone in a sheet of brown mailing paper. Glue
   the overlapping edges together, and push the loose edges
   inside the open ends of the cone. This is the head.
3. For the horns, cut two pieces of brown paper about 2½
   x 1½ inches (6 x 4 cm). Roll each one into a small cone,
   with one corner of the rectangle forming the point. Glue
   closed. Make several cuts around the open ends, and
   bend the flaps outward (Figure 1). Glue the horns to
   the head about 4 inches (10 cm) apart, and the same
   distance from the wide end of the large cone.

49

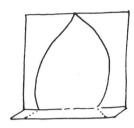

Figure 1   Figure 2

4. Cut two pieces of brown paper 4 inches (10 cm) square, and draw an ear on each one (Figure 2). Cut them out, and fold a small flap along the bottom edge. Spread glue along the flaps, and attach the ears to the head, one on each side of the horns.

5. Cut two oval shapes of white paper or felt, about 1½ inches (4 cm) wide and 3 inches (7.5 cm) long. Glue them to the head to make the eyes. For pupils, cut two smaller ovals of black paper or felt, and glue them on top.

6. Glue the block of styrofoam to the underside of the head. Position it directly beneath the ears.

7. Cut a large rectangle of brown paper, 52 inches (132 cm) long and 36 inches (90 cm) wide. (Glue two or more pieces together, if necessary.)

8. Glue the long edges of the paper together to make a tube for the giraffe's neck.

9. Cut several slits about 4 inches (10 cm) long and 1 inch (2.5 cm) apart around one end of the long paper tube. Bend the pieces between the slits outward to make tabs.

10. Attach the long neck to the head by gluing the tabs to the head in a circle around the styrofoam block. Overlap

50

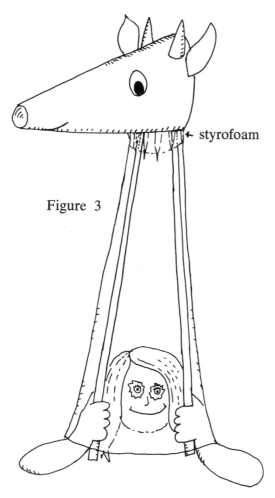

styrofoam

Figure 3

the tabs, if necessary, to make them fit on without making the neck too wide (Figure 3).

11. Cut two eye holes in the front of the neck, 10 inches (26 cm) from the bottom and as far apart as your own.

12. Slip the canes down inside the neck, and push them firmly into the styrofoam block, one underneath each horn.

13. Paint the head and face with irregularly-shaped spots of yellow and brown poster paint, making the spots larger at the bottom of the neck and smaller at the top.

51

MAGICIAN

A magician must keep up a constant flow of jokes and chatter to distract the audience from the "magic" being performed. Try it. It is not as easy as it sounds. You also need to know a few magic words. If "presto" and "Abracadabra" seem a little dull, make up some magic phrases of your own.

HOCUS POCUS CHIMINEE YOCUS

- **MATERIALS**

  sheet of white construction paper, 32 x 20 inches (80 x 50 cm)

  circle of black construction paper, about 20 inches (50 cm) in diameter

  dinner plate, about 12 inches (30 cm) in diameter (or a 6-inch compass, see p. 9)

  strip of black construction paper, 9 x 2 inches (22 x 5 cm)

  glue

  paper fastener

  sharp-pointed scissors

  short piece of cellophane tape

  pencil

  black felt-tip pen

  black poster paint

  paintbrush

  toy rabbit, bunch of paper flowers, or a silk scarf or two

1. Place the dinner plate in the center of the construction paper circle. Draw around the plate, and cut out the circle.
2. With closed scissors, punch a hole in the corners of either long side of the white construction paper. Roll the paper into a tube, and hold the top edges together with a paper fastener through the holes (Figure 1).
3. Put your head through the black paper ring, then put the tube over your head. Overlap the bottom edges of the tube, and press them together so that the tube becomes much narrower at the bottom than at the top.

53

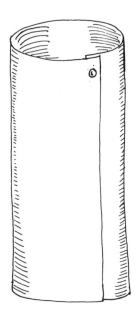

Figure 1

4. Pull the paper ring up over the tube to make the brim of the hat. Ask a friend to mark its position on the tube. Gently mark the position of your eyes.

5. Take the tube and paper ring off your head. Remove the brim and paper fastener, and lay the white construction paper flat. Paint the paper black above the line marked for the brim.

6. Draw the magician's eyes, eyebrows, nose, and mouth in felt-tip pen. Draw in some hair and the outline of the face, and cut holes for the eyes (Figure 2).

7. Draw the shape of a large, handlebar moustache on the strip of black paper. Cut it out, and glue only the center of it under the magician's nose.

8. When the paint is quite dry, roll the paper into the tube and slide the ring back on once more. This time, wedge the ring in position on the tube and tape the top corners of the tube closed.

Figure 2

9. Place the tube on your head. Put the toy rabbit, flowers, scarves, or whatever you prefer inside the hat, so you can surprise your audience when you draw them out with a flourish.

MARTIAN

Would a Martian speak an earthly language? Probably
not, so try to make up a special, outer-space language
to fit this disguise.

• **MATERIALS**

silver, cream eye shadow
cream eye shadow or finger paints, in several colors
fine paintbrush for drawing makeup lines
about 10 bobby pins (or 20 if you have short hair)
elastic band (if you have long hair)
aluminum foil
sharp-pointed scissors
ruler
cellophane tape
piece of string or yarn,
    about 16 inches (30 cm) long

1. If you have long hair, comb it back off your face, and arrange it in a pony tail on top of your head. If you have short hair, comb it back off your face, and hold it back with a line of bobby pins.
2. Cover your face, neck, and ears with silver eye shadow. Make sure your lips and eyebrows are covered, too.
3. Using colorful eye shadow (or the finger paints) and a paintbrush, draw the outline of wide curving lips with drooping corners. Make the drawn lips larger and wider than your own, and do not fill in the outline.
4. Paint squiggles and patterns on your cheeks and forehead using whichever colors you like.
5. Paint the outline of your eyes and long, slanting eyebrows with more eye shadow. Draw pointed corners out the sides of each eye.
6. Cut the foil into strips about 1 inch (2.5 cm) wide and 24 inches (60 cm) long. You will need about thirty for the hair, and another ten for the decoration around the neck.
7. Holding the middle of one of the strips in one hand,

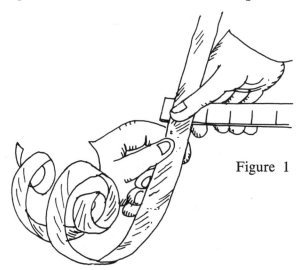

Figure 1

sandwich it between the edge of the ruler and the thumb of your other hand. Pull the strip through between your thumb and the ruler to curl it. Repeat this with the other end of the strip so that it is curled at each end with a straight section in the middle (Figure 1).

8. Curl all the other strips in the same way.

9. With closed scissors, poke a hole in the center of three of the strips, and slide them onto a bobby pin. Repeat this until you have only ten strips left. Place the pins in your hair, and scatter them all over your head so the curls hide your own hair.

10. Lay the remaining ten curled strips side by side on a flat surface with a little gap between each one. Take a piece of cellophane tape, and lay it face down across the center of the strips.

11. Flip the taped foil over, and center the yarn or string on top the tape. Press down so the tape sticks to the yarn or string (Figure 2).

12. Tie the yarn or string around your neck so that your face is completely framed with silver curls.

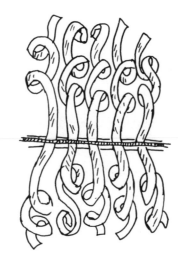

Figure 2

MONSTER

Here you can really let your imagination run wild.
Model the face after your favorite monster, and add
finishing touches, like sharp teeth, as you wish.

• MATERIALS

piece of burlap or loosely-woven fabric, 18 inches (45 cm) square

powder starch used for clothes

bowl

spoon

2 cups water

large balloon

scissors

glue

old saucer

black, dark grey, or dark brown eye shadow

1. Fray the edges of the burlap by pulling out loose threads all around the fabric. Continue until you have made a fringed edge 3 inches (7.5 cm) wide. Keep all the threads you remove.
2. Mix the starch in the bowl, using 2 cups water and twice as much starch for this amount of water as the instructions suggest.
3. Blow up the balloon to the size of your head. This is the "mold" for the monster mask.
4. Dip the piece of burlap in the starch, and drape it over the balloon (Figure 1).
5. Pinch the burlap here and there to make wrinkles. Cut small eye holes, and pull away some of the threads around the eyes. (The more ragged the holes look, the better.)
6. Pick up half the threads from the fringe, and lay them

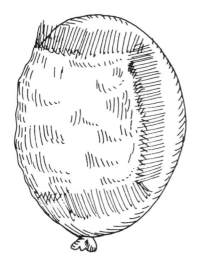

Figure 1

Figure 2

on the mask any way you please. Shape the loose ends around the mask to form a decorative, uneven edge.

7. Let the mask dry overnight before lifting it off the balloon.

8. Pour some glue into an old saucer. Set aside two long pieces, then cut up the remaining threads from the fringe into pieces about 6 inches (15 cm) long. Dip them in the glue, and flop them onto the mask. The messier it looks, the wilder the monster will be. Build up high cheekbones, a huge nose, or add warts or other monster features as you wish (Figure 2).

9. Tie one long thread to loose threads on each side of the mask. Set aside to dry once more. Then put on the mask, and tie the long threads behind your head.

MOTH

This moth disguise is a pair of super sunglasses.
When you put them on,
try to become
light and graceful,
and make fluttering
actions with your hands.

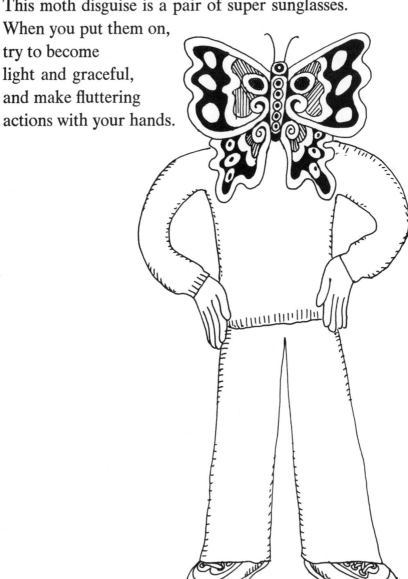

• MATERIALS

piece of white cardboard, about 26 x 20 inches (65 x 50 cm)

piece of newspaper, 20 x 16 inches (50 x 40 cm)

water colors or poster paints

paintbrush

pencil

sharp-pointed scissors

glue

scraps of colored cellophane, acetate, tissue paper, and foil

tape measure

piece of wire, about 12 inches (30 cm) long

small piece of cellophane tape

1. Trim the cardboard to 20 x 16 inches (50 x 40 cm), and save the extra piece.
2. Draw an extra-large moth shape on the newspaper. Give it a cigar-shaped body, and make the top wings larger than the bottom ones. Give the wings a frilly outline, using Figure 1 as a guide. Fold the moth shape in half, and cut out the two sides at the same time so that they match exactly.

Figure 1

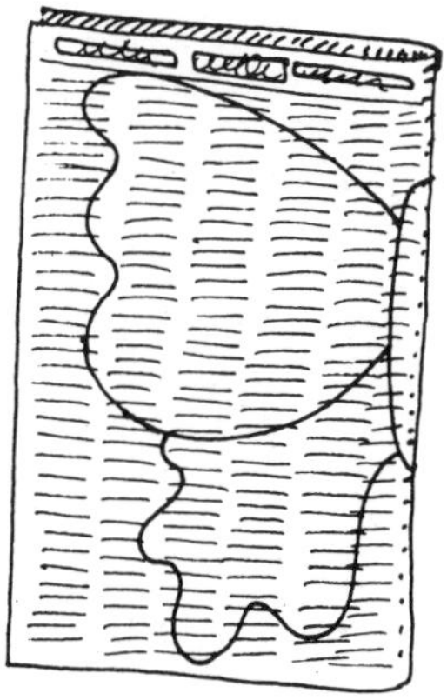

3. Open the newspaper, and trace the shape onto the larger piece of cardboard. Cut it out.
4. Draw the moth markings on the cardboard with pencil (Figure 2).

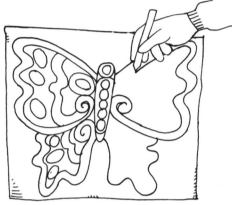

Figure 2

5. Cut out holes for some of the markings, but make sure they are no larger than your scraps of paper. In the middle of the moth, cut out two eye holes.
6. On the wrong side of the moth, spread glue around the edge of each hole and glue a scrap of paper or foil over it. Use transparent papers for the eye holes.
7. Use paint to fill in the rest of the moth markings.
8. Bend the piece of wire in half, and curve the ends to make antennae. Attach it to the wrong side of the moth with cellophane tape. (Figure 3).

Figure 3

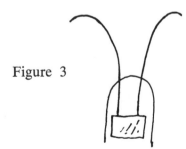

9. From the extra cardboard, cut a small rectangle 4 x 2 inches (10 x 5 cm). Make a cut 1 inch (2.5 cm) long in the center of one of the long sides.

10. Fold the rectangle in half, long edges together. Fold it in half again, short sides together and away from the cut. This is the nose rest (Figure 4).

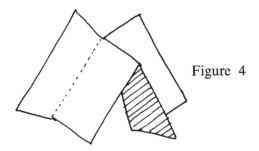

Figure 4

11. Glue the nose rest to the middle of the back of the moth and even with the eye holes.

12. Draw two shapes on the extra cardboard like large letter J's to act as supports for the glasses. The straight part should be as long as the distance from the outer edge of your eye to the middle of your ear, plus 1 inch (2.5 cm). The curved part should be large enough to hook over your ear. Cut out the shapes.

13. Bend back the extra inch (2.5 cm) of the supports, and glue them to the wrong side of the moth, placing them right next to the eye holes.

• **VARIATIONS**

This is an imaginary moth, but why not base the design on a real one? Look in a book on butterflies and moths for ideas.

There is no need to use only moth shapes. Make a really fantastic design with cardboard frames and cellophane lenses—a pair of peacocks, perhaps, a person on a bicycle, or headgear for astronauts or deep-sea divers. The possibilities are endless.

OGRE

Ogres are giants with a taste for human blood. To give other people the right idea, you might carry an old doll without a head and munch suggestively. Like the giant in *Jack and the Beanstalk,* you could mutter, "Fee, fi, fo, fum, I smell the blood of an Englishman."

FEE FI FO FUM YUM YUM YUM YUM

- **MATERIALS**

  cotton
  small lump of plasticine, Play Doh, or nose putty
  old nylon stocking
  scissors
  crochet hook
  red lipstick
  black wax crayon
  nontoxic, white glue or spirit gum
  several bristles from an old brush
  2 strips of bandage tape, 2½ inches (6 cm) long

1. Tie a knot in the stocking near the heel. Cut off the foot, and then cut off the leg 10 inches (25 cm) from the knot.

2. Turn the piece of stocking inside out, and pull it onto your head, tucking your hair underneath. With a crochet hook pull little wisps of hair through the stocking so that it looks as if most of your hair has fallen out, and only a few wisps are left. (If you have long hair, just pull **up** some short loops rather than very long wisps.)

3. Make a pad of cotton large enough to fit over one eye and hold it in place with the strips of bandage tape.

4. Using red lipstick, draw the line of a scar from the top of your forehead down to the top of the cotton. Then continue it below the pad, taking it down across your cheek. Draw some stitch marks across it from side to side.

5. Mold the plasticine, Play Doh, or nose putty into balls

of various sizes to use as warts. Use spirit gum or non-toxic, white glue to glue them in clusters on your cheeks and chin. Glue an extra large one on the end of your nose. (The glue will wash off easily with soap and water, but be careful not to apply it too close to your eyes, mouth, or inside of your nose.)

6. Make the warts look extra ugly by pushing a few stiff bristles into some of them.

7. Use the wax crayon to black out one or two teeth, and make others look jagged or broken.

8. Slip a piece of cotton between your teeth and cheek on each side to make your cheeks look fat and puffy.

OLD MAN

Will you be a grumpy, old man, or the kind, grandfatherly
type? Whichever you choose, walk slowly with a
hunched back and a borrowed cane.

TAP
TAP
TAP

• MATERIALS

skin-colored, thin plastic or rubber bathing cap
1 ounce (25 gm) packet of lamb's wool
talcum powder
small ball of cotton
tissue
scissors
pale foundation makeup
soft, grey eyebrow pencil
wide-toothed comb
glue
piece of narrow ribbon or yarn, at least 16 inches (40 cm) long

1. Cut a piece of lamb's wool 8 inches (20 cm) long, and spread the strands apart sideways to form a square.
2. Spread glue along the center 8 inches (20 cm) of the ribbon or yarn, and lay it in a slightly curved shape across the top edge of the lamb's wool. Trim away the lamb's wool above the ribbon (Figure 1).

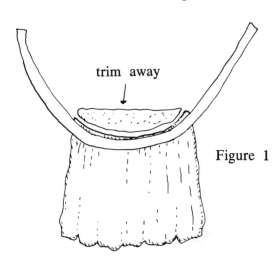

trim away

Figure 1

3. Hold the beard in position beneath your lower lip, and tie the ends of the ribbon behind your head.

4. Spread pale-colored foundation all over your face and lips.

5. Pull on the bathing cap, making sure it comes down onto your forehead, and tuck your hair underneath it.

6. Frown fiercely, and mark three of the horizontal frown lines across your forehead with eyebrow pencil. The lines should be at least ¼ inch (6 mm) apart.

7. Squint your eyes, and with the eyebrow pencil mark three crow's feet from the outer corner of each eye.

8. Using the cotton ball as a puff, powder your eyebrows heavily with talcum powder to turn them pale. Whisk off any surplus powder from your cheeks with a tissue.

9. Cut two pieces of lamb's wool, each about 8 inches (20 cm) long. Lay them side by side, and spread the strands apart sideways until the width has been stretched to 14 inches (35 cm).

10. Leaving the top of the head bald, glue the thinned-out hair around the sides and back of your head, starting and finishing just above your ears. Ask a friend to help you, if necessary, and hold the hair in place for a minute or two until the glue has set.

11. Decide whether you would like your hair to be left as wild and straggly as possible, or neat and tidy with short hair and a pointed beard. Comb the hair gently, and trim it to shape.

OLD WOMAN

See if you can find a shawl or an old baby blanket to
wrap around your shoulders, and then sit huddled up
inside it as if you are cold. Perhaps your old woman
can borrow some knitting to hold, and to peer at
shortsightedly through her glasses.

• MATERIALS

lace-trimmed shower cap
talcum powder and powder puff
bobby pins
comb
pale foundation makeup
grey eyebrow pencil
grey eye shadow
strip of grey construction paper, about 18 inches (45
    cm) long and 2 inches (5 cm) wide
pencil

1. Backcomb your hair at the front and sides, and powder it quite heavily with talcum powder to turn it white or grey. (It will brush out afterward.) If you have dark eyebrows, carefully powder them, too.
2. Bend your hair back in a large wave all around your head, and hold it in place with a line of bobby pins about 3 inches (7.5 cm) back from your hairline.
3. Put on the shower cap, leaving the wave of greyish-white hair showing at the front and sides, but covering the pins.
4. Cover your face and lips with a pale-colored makeup foundation.
5. Use the grey eyeshadow to make shadows *under* your eyes. Suck in your cheeks to see where the hollows come, and add shadows there, too. Blend in all the edges carefully.
6. Frown fiercely, and mark two or three of the frown lines on your forehead with eyebrow pencil.

7. Squint your eyes, and mark the crow's feet with grey pencil, too.
8. With the same pencil, draw any other lines or wrinkles you can find—over your nose, from the sides of your nose to the outer edges of your mouth, and between your lower lip and chin.
9. Purse your lips tightly, and see how they make small vertical wrinkles. Draw in these wrinkles on both your upper and lower lips with eyebrow pencil.
10. Using a pair of sunglasses or regular glasses as a guide, draw the outline of a pair of glasses on the construction paper. Start with the bridge of the nose in the center of the glasses and work outward, making the two sides mirror each other (Figure 1). Turn the real glasses on their side, and draw the ear pieces so that they stick out straight from each paper lens.

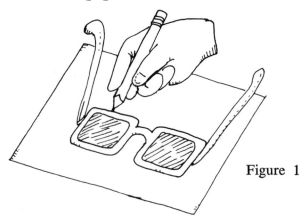

Figure 1

11. Cut out the paper glasses, keeping the frames as narrow and delicate as you can. Fold the paper where the hinges of the glasses should be. Perch the glasses on the end of your nose.

OWL

Have you noticed how an owl moves its head? It moves in short jerks, and can turn its head to face in the opposite direction without turning its shoulders as well. You will not be able to do this, but you will be able to imitate an owl's unblinking stare and eerie hooting call.

HOOT
HOOT

Exotic Variation

• MATERIALS

piece of white construction paper, about 12 x 8 inches
(30 x 20 cm)
lots of feathers collected from outdoors, or several strips
of paper, 3 inches (7.5 cm) long and 1 inch (2.5 cm)
wide, some white and some brown
scraps of shiny black paper
scraps of shiny gold paper
piece of yellow construction paper, 5 x 2½ inches (13
x 7.5 cm)
glue
2 pieces of string, about 18 inches (45 cm) long
compass (see p. 9)
pencil
sharp-pointed scissors

1. With the compass, draw two circles with a radius of 3
   inches (7.5 cm) on the white construction paper, letting
   them overlap ¾ inch (2 cm). Mark the position of your
   eyes on each side of the overlap.
2. Cut around the outer edge of the shape you have drawn,
   leaving the two circles joined together (Figure 1).

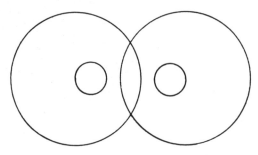

Figure 1

3. Fold the piece of yellow construction paper in half, short edges together. Draw the shape of a hooked beak on one side, making it as large as you can (Figure 2). Cut it out, cutting through two thicknesses of paper.

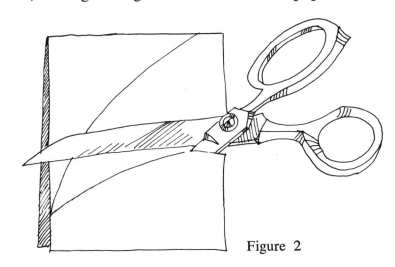

Figure 2

4. Glue the two beak shapes together only along the long curved edge. Set the beak aside to dry.

5. Draw two circles with a radius of ¾ inch (2 cm), and two with a radius of ¼ inch (6 mm) on the shiny black paper. Cut them out.

6. Draw two circles with a radius of ½ inch (12 mm) on the shiny gold paper. Cut them out.

7. Divide the paper circles into two identical sets. Glue them one on top of the other, working from large to small. Then glue them into position on the mask to make the eyes. Carefully slit the center of each eye with the point of the scissors.

8. Cut the top 3 inches (7.5 cm) off each of the feathers, and discard the rest. If you are using paper strips in-

stead, cut one long edge into a fringe. (Cut several strips at once to save time.)

9. Glue a ring of pale-colored feathers (or white paper strips) around the outer edge of the mask, and also down the center between the eyes. Position them so that the fluffy tips of the feathers and fringed edges of the paper overlap each other and the edges of the mask.

10. Add a ring of dark-colored feathers (or paper strips) inside the pale ones in the same way, letting them overlap each other.

11. Fill in the rest of the area with pale-colored feathers (or fringed paper strips).

12. Make a mark on the short curved edge of each side of the beak ½ inch (12 mm) from the straight edge. Draw a straight line from the top corner to this mark on each side (Figure 3). Fold the paper outward along the lines to make tabs on each side of the beak. Pull the sides of the beak apart a little, and position beneath the eyes. Glue the tabs to the wrong side of the mask.

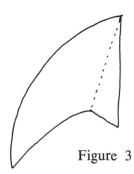

Figure 3

13. With the point of the scissors, make a hole on each side of the mask near the outer edges, and tie a piece of string

to each one. Fit the beak over your nose, and tie the strings behind your head.

- **VARIATIONS**

The colors used in this mask are right for a hawk owl. However, you can make a snowy owl disguise all in white, or a grey owl in shades of grey, white, and brown. Or use painted feathers and bright paper to make an exotic imaginary bird in colors of your choice.

PHARAOH

Pharaohs always looked serious and superior, so look very solemn and remember not to smile. Their cosmetics were usually highly perfumed, so why not put on some perfume yourself to create the right kind of atmosphere?

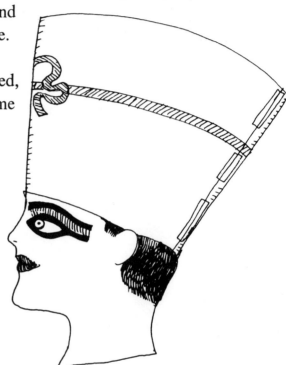

- **MATERIALS**

construction paper, 26 x 10 inches (66 x 25 cm), any
  color
metallic gold paper, 26 x 10 inches (66 x 25 cm)
piece of binding or ribbon, 30 inches (75 cm) long
paper clip
glue
small piece of cellophane tape
piece of thick cord, about 12 inches (30 cm) long
elastic band

82

several bobby pins
comb
shiny gold, cream eye shadow
blue or green, cream eye shadow (or both)
black, liquid eye liner and brush
red lipstick
perfume, with a touch of Egypt about it

1. Stiffen the sheet of gold paper by gluing it onto the construction paper.
2. Glue the binding or ribbon to the paper about 3 inches (7.5 cm) from one long edge. This will be the top edge of the headdress.
3. Bend the cord into a clover leaf shape, and glue it onto the binding halfway from each end (Figure 1).

Figure 1

4. Comb your hair off your face and, if it is long enough, fix it in a pony tail on the top of your head. Put in a row of bobby pins all around your head about 1 inch (2.5 cm) from your hairline.

5. Bend the gold paper around your head so that it fits tightly around your hairline, with overlapping ends in front. Clip the overlapping bottom edges together temporarily with a paper clip. Pull the upper edges apart a little, so that the headdress becomes wider toward the top. Secure both the top and bottom edges with tape, and remove the paper clip.

6. Turn the headdress so that the cord decoration is in front. Make sure that no wisps of hair escape from beneath it.

7. Cover your whole face, neck, and ears with gold eye shadow.

8. Using black eye liner and starting at the inner corner of one eye, draw a line along the edge of your upper eyelid, extending it for ¾ inch (2 cm) in a straight line at the outer corner. Draw a second line as close as you can beneath your eye.

9. Again with black eye liner, draw a thick, straight eyebrow parallel to the line on the upper eyelid, and extending out to the side to match it.

10. Spread blue or green eyeshadow on your upper eyelid between the eyeline and the eyebrow. (You can follow Cleopatra's example and use deep blue on your upper lids and bright green on your lower lids.)

11. Make up your other eye to match.

12. Make your lips full and red with the lipstick.

84

PIRATE

If you have read *Treasure Island* recently, you are sure
to remember the pirate song beginning, "Fifteen men
on a dead man's chest." Cultivate a gruff voice, add a
few "Yo heave ho's," and remember to scowl fiercely.

• MATERIALS

small piece of black cardboard, about 3 inches (7.5 cm) square

piece of black elastic, about 20 inches (50 cm) long

striped sock or stocking

large colored handkerchief

large metal curtain ring

thread

black finger paint (or greasepaint *), or a soft, black eyebrow pencil

collodion or New-Skin, or a soft, brown eyebrow pencil

red and blue powder or poster paints and brush, or a packet of "painless tattoos" (transfers)

1. Ruffle up your hair to make it look really wild and unkempt.
2. Pull the sock or stocking onto your head to act as a cap, leaving plenty of hair sticking out all around. If it is long enough, tie a knot near the ankle to disguise the shape of the foot.
3. Knot the handkerchief around your neck.
4. If you have some collodion or New-Skin, paint a stripe down one cheek from the outer edge of your eye to your mouth. When it is dry, open your mouth as wide as you can so that you stretch your cheek. Your skin will pucker to look like a scar when you close your mouth again. Or draw the line of a scar with pale brown eyebrow pencil. Make pairs of dots, one on either side of the line, to look like the holes where the stitches were made.

5. Tie the curtain ring on a loop of thread, and hang it over your ear on the same side as the scar (Figure 1).

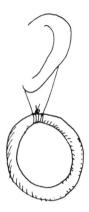

Figure 1

6. Trim the corners of the piece of cardboard into curves. Make a hole in each of the top corners. Thread the elastic through them, and tie the ends behind your head (Figure 2). Wear the eye patch on the opposite side of your face from the scar.

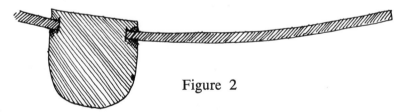

Figure 2

7. Draw a moustache with black finger paint, greasepaint, or black eyebrow pencil. Draw it with short strokes sloping down and out toward the sides of your face. This will look much more realistic than an outline filled in with solid color.

8. For the finishing touch, put a "painless tattoo" on the back of each hand, or draw them using dotted lines of powder or poster paint (Figure 3).

Figure 3

PRINCE CHARMING

In order to give the impression
that you have stepped
straight out of a
fairy tale, practice
walking lightly and
daintily, your back straight
and head held high.
You are used to pointing
your toes in a courtly
minuet, and to bowing
gracefully to all
the ladies. You might
carry with you
a high-heeled shoe
covered with silver foil
to show that you are
searching for your
own Cinderella.

89

• MATERIALS

cheap, rubber swimming cap
small package rolled, first aid cotton
2-inch (5-cm) wide black ribbon, 24 inches (60 cm)
   long
talcum powder and powder puff
blusher
lipstick
scissors
tape measure
football or a wig stand, or a friend to act as one
rectangle of colored cardboard, 7 x 3 inches (18 x 7.5
   cm)
garden cane or wooden dowel, 14 inches (36 cm) long
few sequins, beads, or other decoration

1. Put the cap on a football, wig stand, or a patient friend
   while you turn it into a wig.
2. Glue a long, wide strip of cotton around the edge of the
   cap so that it hangs over at the front by about 2 inches
   (5 cm). Turn back the overlapping cotton at the front,
   and glue it in place.
3. Fill in the gap in the back of the crown with another
   piece of cotton.
4. Cut eight strips of cotton, 2½ inches (7 cm) wide and
   5 inches (13 cm) long. Roll them into sausage shapes,
   and glue four on each side of the head. Place them horizontally, one above the other. Make sure the two sides
   are the same (Figure 1).

90

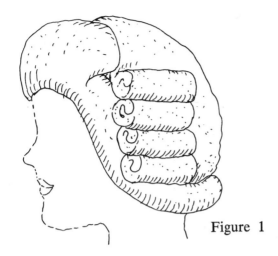

Figure 1

5. Tie the ribbon in a bow, and glue it to the back of the wig at the nape (base) of the neck (Figure 2).

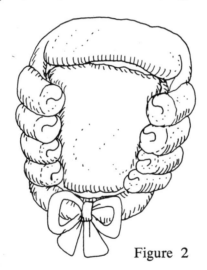

Figure 2

6. Put on the wig, tucking all your own hair inside it.
7. Powder your face with a little talcum powder to make it look pale.
8. Rub in a small amount of blusher (or lipstick) on each cheekbone. Then paint your lips with lipstick.

9. Cut the colored cardboard into a large figure 8. The holes should be the same distance apart as your eyes. Used horizontally, this becomes a mask.

10. Glue the end of the cane to one side of the mask (Figure 3).

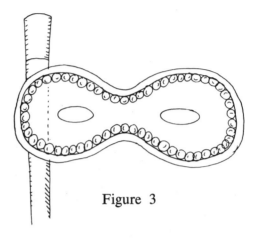

Figure 3

11. Glue the sequins or other decoration around the edge of the mask, and Prince Charming is ready for the ball.

ROBOT

If your robot can talk, it will
probably be in a high-pitched
monotone. And, of course,
it will walk very slowly,
stiffly, and unnaturally,
more like a machine
than a human.

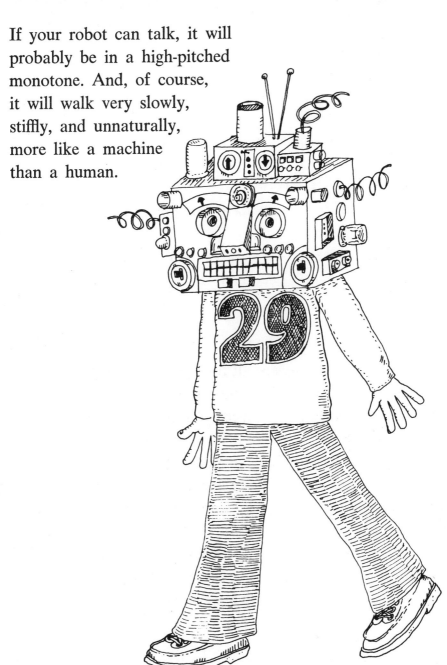

cardboard carton, large enough to fit over your head

selection of odd-shaped boxes, packaging, and cardboard tubes

selection of old bottle tops and tin can lids

pieces of scrap or junk—such as springs, pieces of wire, beads, spools

scraps of transparent paper

glue

sharp-pointed scissors

grey latex paint (or black poster paint mixed with a little white latex)

model enamel in any color(s) you choose

2 paintbrushes—one about 1 inch (2.5 cm) wide, and one smaller

pencil

1. There are no rules at all for this disguise. Just let your imagination run wild, and try to find a use for all the odd-shaped bits and pieces you have collected.
2. Put the carton over your head, and mark the eye holes with the pencil. Remove the carton, and cut two eye holes or one rectangular panel to see through.
3. Start with the large boxes and pieces of junk, and glue them onto the carton to make all kinds of control panels. Cut holes in any boxes you stick over the eye holes, or fit cardboard tubes into the holes instead. Perhaps your robot has a tall, complicated superstructure with lots of boxes piled on top. Perhaps it is unable to turn its head,

and literally needs eyes and other controls in the back of its head as well.

4. Perhaps your robot has feelers or antennae of wire. Attach them by bending one end around a spool or a small box, and then gluing the spool or box to the carton. Bend the other end around a small bead, or push a small ball of foil onto the tip so there is no danger of it scratching anyone.

5. Paint the whole robot head grey.

6. When the paint is dry, glue on the smaller bits and pieces, such as bottle tops and buttons, for the smaller switches and controls. Perhaps their colors are all right as they are, or perhaps you will want to paint them with enamel.

7. If the eye holes have not been fitted with tubes or boxes, glue pieces of transparent paper to cover them.

SANTA CLAUS

• MATERIALS

piece of red crepe paper, 25 x 20 inches (63 x 50 cm)
double-sided cellophane tape
small package rolled, first aid cotton
red lipstick or blusher
rubber band
scissors
4 bobby pins

1. Lay the paper flat on your work surface. Fold the long edges in toward the middle so that they overlap about 1 inch (2.5 cm). Hold the overlapping edges together by sandwiching a strip of double-sided tape between them. You now have a paper tube.

2. Gather one of the open ends of the tube and hold it closed with the rubber band to form Santa's cap. Tape a ball of cotton on this closed end. Around the opposite open end, attach a strip of double-sided tape, peel off the backing, and press pieces of cotton onto it to make the trim.

3. Rub some lipstick or blusher on your cheeks and also on the end of your nose so that it looks as if you have just come in from the cold.

4. Cut two strips of tape 2½ inches (6 cm) long, and press a piece of cotton onto each. Cut the cotton and tape together into crescent shapes. Peel off the backing, and stick the shapes over your own eyebrows.

5. Cut a piece of tape 3 inches (7.5 cm) long for the moustache, and press a strip of cotton onto it. Cutting through tape and cotton together, make a curve in one of the long edges so that it will fit under your nose. Peel off the backing, and stick it in place.

6. Cut two pieces of tape long enough to reach from the side of your head, level with your eye, to just below the corner of your mouth. Peel off the backing, and stick the pieces of tape to your face.

7. Cut a piece of tape long enough to reach from left to right along your chin. Peel off the backing, and stick it to your face.

8. Cut a large piece of cotton 12 inches (30 cm) long and 6 inches (15 cm) wide. Hold the two top corners, and tug gently to widen the top end of the cotton to about 10 inches (26 cm).

9. Cut this top edge into a curve so that it dips about 2 inches (5 cm) in the middle. This makes the beard and sideburns. Press the shaped edge of the wool onto the sticky tape on the sides of your face and your lower lip.

10. Now trim and tidy the beard, moustache, and eyebrows. Start by pulling off little pieces of cotton all around the edges of everything to give a softer, more natural-looking finish. Shape the moustache and eyebrows, twisting the ends between dampened fingers.

11. Put on the cap, and hold it to your hair with bobby pins.

SKELETON

A ghostly skeleton flits silently about, so remember to change out of your hobnailed boots. Wrap a sheet around you, and try to glide across the floor. For the very best effects, light a candle, draw the curtains, and turn out the lights. Stand in a gloomy corner away from the candle, and enjoy the horrified expression of anyone who comes into the room.

• MATERIALS

black poster paint
luminous white, yellow, or silver paint
small paintbrush
black scarf
balloon that will blow up bigger than your head
newspaper
flour-and-water paste (see p. 10)
Vaseline
sharp-pointed scissors
2 pieces of string, about 12 inches (30 cm) long
pencil

1. Blow up the balloon to the size of your head or larger, and tie the neck. Cover it with Vaseline.
2. Tear some newspaper into pieces about 2 inches (5 cm) square. Dip them one by one into the paste, and lay them on the balloon, edges overlapping (Figure 1).

Figure 1

3. Leaving a small space around the neck, cover the balloon with four or five layers of newspaper pieces.
4. Hang the balloon up by the neck, and let it dry. This will take about twenty-four hours.

5. Burst the balloon, and pull it out of the paper shell. Cut around the shape from top to bottom to make two masks. Use the second one for the China Doll disguise (p. 23).

6. Place the mask in front of your face, and make pencil marks where the eyes should be. Remove the mask, and cut two eye slits.

7. With the point of the scissors, make a hole at each side of the mask. Tie a piece of string through each hole.

8. Sketch the outlines of a normal face on the mask in pencil—eyebrows, eyes, nose, mouth.

9. Paint large black eye sockets extending from the line of the eyebrows to the tops of the cheeks. Paint a large black triangle for the nose, leaving a vertical strip in the upper half of the nose unpainted. Add the outline of a very large, wide mouth, much larger than a normal mouth, and also solid triangular shapes for the sunken cheeks.

10. Paint the outline of the teeth inside the mouth. Remember that the upper teeth are larger and wider than the lower ones. Paint a few black spaces for missing teeth.

11. Cover all the unpainted areas with luminous paint.

12. Put on the mask, and tie the strings behind your head. Tie the black scarf around your head to frame the skeleton's face.

WISE MAN FROM THE EAST

As one of the three wise men who came bearing gifts to the infant Jesus, you must walk in a slow, stately fashion so that people immediately realize you are of royal blood. Cover a box or vase with gold or silver foil to look like one of the precious gifts of gold, frankincense, or myrrh.

• MATERIALS

3 teaspoons of cocoa (or a stick of dark tan greasepaint *)
small ball of cotton
cup
spoon
soft, black or brown eyebrow pencil
ball of fine, black yarn
plain white or striped dishtowel
piece of rope or thick cord, about 1½ yards (1.35 m)
  long
safety pin
ruler or tape measure

1. Mix the cocoa with 2 teaspoons of very hot water so
    that it looks like smooth cream. Let it cool.
2. Brush your hair back away from your face. Use the
    cotton ball to dab the cocoa mixture evenly all over your
    face. (Or apply the brown greasepaint.)
3. Squint your eyes, and draw the creases at the outer edges
    with black or dark brown eyebrow pencil.
4. Make your eyebrows darker and bushier with the eye-
    brow pencil. Make short, feathery strokes, not a heavy
    line.
5. Cut one piece of yarn 24 inches (60 cm) long, and tie it
    to the backs of two chairs.
6. Cut at least forty pieces of yarn, each 10 inches (25 cm)
    long, and knot them onto the long piece of yarn. To do
    this, fold each piece in half, hold the loop behind the
    long piece of yarn, and pass the ends through the loop

(Figures 1a-d). Pull the pieces tightly and space them evenly along the center 8 inches (20 cm) of the long piece of yarn.

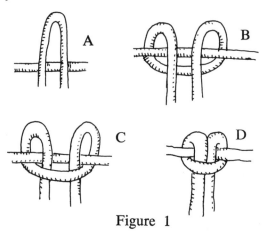

Figure 1

7. Untie the long piece of yarn from the chairs. Hold the center of it just below your lower lip and take the ends back over your ears, tying them at the back of your head (Figure 2).

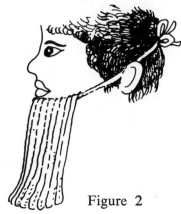

Figure 2

8. Trim the bottom edge of the yarn beard to whatever shape you like.

9. Lay the dishtowel over your head so that one long side hangs down over your forehead. Pin the front edges together under your chin to hide your makeup-free neck.

10. Wind the cord twice around your head over the dishtowel, and tie it in a knot at the back.

• VARIATIONS

Use the same basic disguise for the other two magi. You could make their beards of different colored yarns, or you could make them bushier (more pieces of yarn), longer, or shorter.

Instead of the cord, you could make a paper or cardboard crown to wear over the dishtowel. Or twist the towel up into a turban, and hold the ends with a borrowed brooch or safety pin. Remember to give your neck the cocoa treatment if you do this.

105

WITCH

Think up a few spells to recite and cackle like a mean, old woman as you fly off on your broomstick.

LIZARDS AND RATS WORMS AND BATS

SHARKS AND SNAILS AND ELEPHANT TAILS

• MATERIALS

2 sheets thick, black cardboard, at least 26 x 20 inches
(65 x 50 cm)
1 ball black raffia or thick yarn
white chalk or crayon
cellophane tape
sharp-pointed scissors
several paper clips
plate or saucer, about 5½ inches (14 cm) in diameter
bodkin or large embroidery needle
thumbtack
ballpoint pen
tape measure

1. Roll one of the cardboard rectangles into a cone so that
   one of the corners forms the top point. The opposite
   corner at the open end of the cone also forms a point.
   This point is the witch's chin (Figure 1).

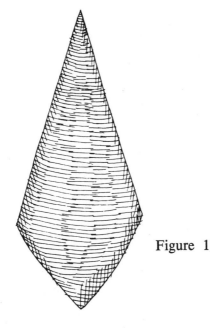

Figure 1

2. Close the overlapping edges of the cone with tape.

3. Fold the second piece of cardboard in half, short sides together. Draw a large circle on it about 13 inches (33 cm) in diameter. (See page 9 for compass instructions.)

4. Cut out the circle, cutting through both thicknesses of cardboard.

5. Place the plate or saucer in the center of each cardboard circle, and draw around it. Cut out the two circles to form the rings for the brim of the hat.

6. Cut the yarn into at least forty pieces, each one 22 inches (55 cm) long. (Cut more pieces for bushier hair.) Tie a knot in one end of each piece.

7. Use the bodkin to thread the yarn pieces through one of the hat brims, pulling them through so that the knots hold them in place. Place them about ½ inch (12 mm) from the inner edge of the brim, and thread all through from the same side (Figure 2). Leave a gap of about 4 inches (20 cm) so that the hair will not hide the witch's face.

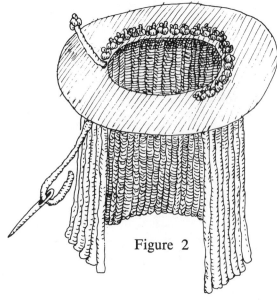

Figure 2

8. Spread glue over the side of the brim with all the knots, making sure that it goes right up to the edges of the cardboard. Lay the second brim on top so that the knots are sandwiched between them. Slip paper clips onto both edges to hold the layers together until the glue has dried.

9. Remove the paper clips and fit the brim onto the cone. Make sure the gap in the hair is at the front.

10. Try on the disguise, and mark it for eye holes. Remove it again, and cut two eye slits.

11. Draw eyebrows, a nose, and a mouth in white crayon or chalk. Make the features angular, and as exaggerated and frightening as you like.

INDEX

ABOUT THE AUTHOR

Eve Barwell, an imaginative and talented craftsperson, is a native of England and a graduate of the University of London. She has worked with craft books for children both as an editor and as an author. *Make Your Pet a Present,* published by Lothrop, was her first book for the American market.

Ms. Barwell lives in London, where she is a freelance editor and writer. In her spare time, she likes to travel to "somewhere hot in Europe" and experiment with "anything and everything crafty."